AF145048

Stamatios Paraskevas

The Enlightenment

THE

ENLIGHTENMENT

New perspective

APHORISMS

by Stamatios Paraskevas

TWENTYSIX
Eine Marke der Books on Demand GmbH
© 2023, Stamatios Paraskevas
Production and publishing:
BoD - Books on Demand, Norderstedt.

ISBN: 9783740781521

PREVIEW

The left-hand pages are blank so that
readers can jot down their own
thoughts there.

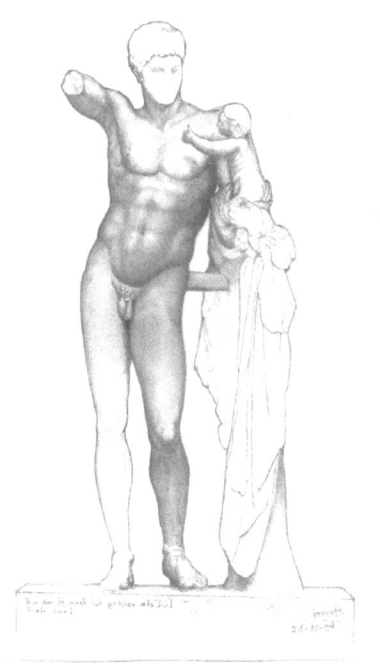

Only the sky is bigger than you, look!

Someone once said, everything has somehow already been said, one way or another, and you can endure life as long as you don't understand it. That can't be. There must be another level on which you can live when you have understood. You are born, you are told, you are given life, whereas the only thing you are given is death, because whether you will live you do not know, but that you will die, that is certain. I'm changing from one subject to another, yes?

I perceive, therefore I exist, I think, therefore I give form, I shape!

The body is not the house, but the inside of the house.

Imagine a straw in a glass of water, the straw is the body and the water is the energy that is in you and around you, that is your true nature!!!

The human being is an energy field, a sphere.

Incidentally, an explosion was recently observed in the universe that formed a perfect spherical shape. There is no explanation for it. Do the universe and people shape each other?

Do you need a god? I am
at your disposal!

OR: Caiaphas asked Jesus, are you a god? He answered, you said so!

But Jesus thought, I am available so that the prophecy is not lost!

HA! HA!

What is paradise for you is hell for me. I can't imagine dawdling around like a stupid angel instead of travelling around to the galaxies, to the true paradise, taking on new life forms, and so on.

What is the real hell for me: meeting you all again! No matter where!

After this life, of course!

—

Time begins with you and ends with
you. In the meantime, you can be
God. But you hide behind what you
do, work!
Isn't that a shame?

There are many Homo sapiens
but few Anthropos (human
beings), that lies in coma
unfortunately in you.
Sometimes he makes himself heard,
but you don't hear his voice.

For most people only exist but do
not live.

What you have made familiar to yourself, you are responsible for YOUR rose, each one for his. It can be anything you have familiarised yourself with in the course of your life, e.g. knowledge.

I have killed the snake, this monster of energy. The way is clear!!!

Namely, the snake (which, by the way, is seven miles long), which is mentioned in all cultures and religions. It is the energy monster that awaits us after this life, as seen by the shamans, the sorcerers of all tribes, e.g. in China, in ancient Greece, in Egypt, by the American Indians (Hopi, Incas).

You do not become a human being, you are born as one.

But you are not born a Greek, a German, but a human being, you are brought up as a Greek, a German, a Christian, a Muslim, etc.!!!

———

How are we all being educated? The question arises, what is education and what is missionary work, the boundaries become mixed and education becomes chaotic. Think about it, Homo sapiens!

I am a serious man and live a
ridiculous life, contemplating the
serious life of ridiculous men.

Take time every day to sit still and listen to things.

Pay attention to the melody of life that resonates within you.

And do the deed.

The reality of the true man is
active, something becoming, even
when he is at rest,

instead

the reality of most is static, fixed,
stuck, even when they seem to be
active.

—

When I exploded into a thousand pieces, I was in the world instead of just looking at it.

I was not made of solid matter, or rather, I was made of the non-fabric. Tao.

What are they doing to our Mother Earth!

Because the earth had a soul long before
we Homo sapiens appeared. Everything
has a soul.

After all the interbreeding of all human-like species (e.g. Neanderthal man merged with Homo sapiens, etc.). By the way, the Neanderthal man was created by the same God as us, image of God too, think about that.

We know about them, but they didn't know about each other. They thought a bad-looking person was the Neanderthal, but a person. And now we all have 3% of them because they did the most natural thing, fell in love with each other. And we're still sitting there and we're talking about races, nations and religions. Yet the whole thing is just a matter of framing.

Note
Frame: Framework in life (microcosm), universe(macrocosm).

We live in a globalised world, that
of the pundits idiots!!!

———

Life is an explosion, afterwards you
are in the world instead of just
looking at it!!!

And anything is possible!!!

———

Tell me, have I played my part well
in this comedy called life?

———

I didn't know that they knew that I
didn't know that they knew what I
was thinking. Telepathy.

Deeply they wanted to bury me,
but they forgot that I am a seed.

I have nothing to do right now, but
if you need a god, I'm available! HA!

So much for Christianity!

Prophecy: If the whole world comes together in this happy moment, namely in the same second all creatures shit, experience this poignant moment of liberation, it will be enlightened!!! HA!

So much for Buddhism.

When the Muslim enters paradise,
he gets ten virgins. If he fucks them,
they become common cunts. For all
eternity!!! HA!

So much for Islam.

—

Jesus' holy mother was a virgin
lesbian who adopted him! HA! HA!
The Sappho of Judea. HA! HA!

What is more natural than that - what?!

Virgin born, either all or none,
Homo sapiens.

Yet there is no paradise, no hell, all
there is is the journey to other
galaxies and on this earth the
promises of Mara, the antagonist of
Buddha.

One thousand four hundred years after
the Old Testament and 600 years after the
birth of Christ came one who claimed to
be the descendant of Ishmael, a man
forgotten in the Old Testament, and he
founded a new religion. He integrated
everything, pagan elements (Meteorite:
Sign of God ,Kaaba), and man's
inclination to violence (Jihad) as well as
testamentary elements and simplified it so
that everyone could understand it. A
genius! His name was Mohammed. 1400
years later!!

(Mohamed is credited with hearing the voice of the
archangel Gabriel and with making a journey to a
"distant cultural site", popularly known as the
Ascension).

Could it be that Mohamed was psychotic despite
or even because of his genius?

Ascension, psychotic episode? Heard the voice of
the Archangel Gabriel, simply heard voices? What
would people say about that nowadays, if he had
lived today. Imagine it!

At that time, schizophrenics were considered
favourites of the gods, others tried to bring
themselves to ecstasy and people could not explain
this state.

The idea of resurrection deserves
respect in itself. And who saw it?
Jesus' life partner, Mary Magdalene,
of course(By the way, only she
understood him). At that time
there were many miracle healers
and saviours, but none who had the
idea of resurrection.
Respect!

Let's take a closer look at Jesus: Did he know how to write and read? He did not write anything himself, that is not mentioned anywhere. That he could tell stories is mentioned, nothing else. An illiterate man, but a good storyteller, all the more respect for his idea(By the way, he also talked to God, simply schizophrenic?). But it is also all the more incredible that so many believe in him. A thousand-and-one-night fairy tale is all I can say.

I am the vibration in space-time!

I exploded, I shrank
and the energy found its way out
through the chest, bubbling, just like
a pulsar microcosm, macrocosm also
the human being.

—

In which God in which universe
should one believe?

———

The cruellest lies are the truths that
are never spoken!

—

Abraham and Moses both heard the voice of God, nowadays we would say that both were simply schizophrenic. So much for Judaism!!! HA!

For the misstep of a minute, you can pay for years.

(Indian saying)

Lotus flowers grew where Buddha stepped, trees where he shit. Strong fertiliser, you see? HA!

Come to Daddy, come to Daddy, he loves you so much!

Said God the Father to Jesus! HA!

How often did Jesus bathe himself?
Once, at his baptism! HA! HA!

I have nothing to do right now, but
if you need a god or prophet, I am
available!
HA! HA! So much for monotheism.

For the schizophrenic Abraham (if he
had lived today, progenitor of
monotheism, c. 1700 BC) heard a voice
when he was alone in the wilderness, and
said to himself: I am alone, who speaks
to me? And behold, so simply was the
presence of God proven. He convinced
himself, so to speak! Laughter. (It was
simply a new idea. Polytheism was
known until then.) So we owe the
presence of God to a schizophrenic
Australopithecus! With the exception of
real humans (e.g.: Empedocles). The
leaps of evolution, it's as simple as that!
(Old Testament around 800 B.C.)

Life expectancy at that time was 30
years and wishful thinking was the
reason for the myth of Abraham
being 170 years old. Just as myths
are created.

Psychedelic: The soul reveals itself.

The only certain thing in this life is that we will die, that the solar system and the whole universe will be destroyed. That is the state of knowledge today. So where is the sense? If not in our sensations, through which we are able to perceive vibrations. The known world of that time had its gods and explanations.

What is a moment worth? The past
is already gone, the future is fantasy,
only the present can be experienced.
In short: everything and nothing!

—

And this paradise, where is it to be? This universe has an end, whether now or in 13 billion years, it has an end. So where is this paradise, it is supposed to last forever. So what is this nonsense?! (Laughter)

Go to paradise! But go right now!
But alone. (Laughter)

Money is a good servant but a bad master!

(Bedouin saying)

There is the reality of most and the inner reality, I have flooded this reality with my reality!!!! I should have taken. What my heart desired!!! Too bad!!

Intuition is direct perception!

It is possible for man to reach the ultimate reality of the universe.

(Upanishad)

Knowledge is action. Knowledge is experience. It does not persist. Its duration is called the moment!

They deprive their own children of the possibility of becoming gods! Or more simply: Buddhas!!! Or more simply: true human beings!!! At least the children who had the misfortune to grow up under the monotheistic dictatorship and with the analogue brainwashing!!!!

Something else: Christians do believe in the resurrection of all Christians, and that presupposes that the bones remain intact. QUESTION: Where are the bones of all Christians for 2000 years and what happens if it takes another 2000/5000 years to happen? Consider how many billions of Christians there are already, and what will become of all those bones? There are already problems with preservation now, let alone in 5000 years. Absurd, isn't it? I'd rather be burned and go into nothingness, which is the destiny of this universe.

—

Living legends become myths,
myths become beliefs, and these
become faith!!!

A lot of shit is done because of
tradition, for example there were
Brahmins and their gods and then
Buddha turned everything upside
down and then he also became
tradition. I think religions also need
renewal (just like art and science),
and all that related to the last 3000-
5000 years. And the rest?

—

John said that Maria said, Michael
said, Peter said, etc., that it
happened that way, that he had
done or told something like that.
Do you understand?!!

By the way, the Romans
persecuted the Jews and
Christians for political and not
religious reasons, so if you
extend the Passion of Christ at
Easter in time to 6 months, the
whole thing takes on a political
dimension. Do you understand?

Demon: Look up what it means in ancient Greek!!! First hint: benevolent deity in Greek mythology. Second: Empedocles (he called himself an immortal benevolent demon). Third: Only afterwards did it become Satan in monotheism.

—

Make up and don't compare
yourselves all the time. That is
the problem!

We will all die one day, one by
one or all at once, what
difference does it make?
The irony is that the planet will
also perish one day, and the
stupid thing is, the war, instead
of making our lives as
comfortable as possible. Do you
see what I mean, Homo sapiens?

What do Adolf Hitler and Jesus have in common? They both took the responsibility upon themselves. One here and the other in the hereafter! (eternal glory, eternal reward)

———

Some think we should leave this
planet; I mean, this universe!

We know that we are dying, we know that humanity will eventually die out. So what is the point? Except that we ourselves travel to other galaxies, universes in the form of consciousness and life force or energy. We are the attempt of matter towards spirit. One way or another!

—

One should live as one can, and not as one wants!

Without ifs and buts !!!

Salvation is won and it is not given!!!

I am lost, I am going to paradise!
Despite the melody of life, I was
bent on GOD. Big mistake.

Tolteke look, a great counter!!!

On the day of the end of oil is the
end of globalisation and civilisation!!!

And what will happen, Buddha,
when humanity becomes
enlightened? Won't all fossil fuels
be burned, won't everything be
destroyed anyway? Isn't the world
doomed? So what is this nonsense?

Imagine humanity is enlightened,
women have taken power, there is
peace, but the world is still ending
because it is caught in the vicious circle
of energy consumption. Who doesn't
want to heat, cook, wash, etc. in
winter? (Industry, cars, planes, oil
tankers, etc.) Climate change is here,
and it is our downfall, one way or
another.Socrates, Jesus and Co. didn't
even know what fossil fuels were, and
the weather was still fine, but today?

It's just madness, just smile that's all
you can do.

We know that the sun will explode at some point and the earth with it. Then we stand there without a point of reference. Where will the resurrection of the dead take place then? And where is paradise supposed to be then? Idiotic! The only thing that makes sense is the journey into other galaxies, into other parallel universes, with their own consciousness and their own life energy!!!

We live in a world without meaning.
Meaning is replaced by classes,
nations, religions, etc. These are all
frameworks that need to be blown
up in order to experience the real
truth!!!!

At the end of this journey of loss, happiness was waiting outside the door. I did not go out.

———

You grow thousands of roses and find nothing. Yet you can find the truth in a single rose and in a little water. The eyes are blind, you have to search with your heart.

———

I had the how and asked
why!!! Stupid, isn't it?

———

The snail went to the cherry tree and
the birds said to her: "You fool, can't
you see that there are no cherries?
And she answered: When I arrive,
there will be some! And she laughed.

———

Salvation itself is also earned and not given.

For an infinite material world leaves no room for an afterlife, since temporal beginninglessness of the universe excludes a creation and its eternal existence excludes a Last Judgement.

Besides, how you can have an Australopithecus as a god is beyond me.

Because God and Australopithecus, that's a conceptual contradiction.

—

With death we come to the original state we were in, before birth! So what is this nonsense?

———

In this infinite space, this universe of infinite galaxies, God dwells with us of all people, in our Milky Way, in our solar system? It is absurd, simply absurd!!!

—

The daddy sent his son, the rest of
the herd of oxen come out of
nowhere!!! HE? HA! And then he
even goes to paradise or hell!!!

———

I defend your rights, I am in
opposition, I shout and I swear, but
the laws are made by others!!!!
YEAH! Am I good or what!!!

———

You can't burn up if you don't have fire in you!!!

———

To one who finds himself, the world is no longer equal!!!

You are not born a Christian, you become one. By the way, just like any other shit, e.g. nationality. But you are born as a human being with all that you carry around with you. What Mother Nature has given you.

—

Eternity lasts as long as the hydrogen in the universe lasts!!!

And the solar system will long cease to exist before that happens. So much for eternity. So what is this nonsense?

———

We humans are magical beings who undertake a journey of consciousness. But we all make the mistake of wanting to interpret everything. Gods, prophets, gurus and masters - everyone tells their crap. What is the use of words when the feeling arises!!! One should pay attention to what one carries within oneself, with oneself!!!

Because we are aware of death, and that distinguishes us from the other animals, and we have only one judge, our conscience, that is all we have.

It's about all of us finally coming to our senses and coexisting with each other. In peace!!

———

Jesus: I think there was also mescaline back then and that's how he had his mind-expanding experiences. Somehow he got to a parallel world where things were peaceful. He had heard about it through the ancient scriptures and did exactly what had been prophesied. A clever man!! But what a trip, and he saw it through to the end, what madness!!!! What a homo sapiens!!!

What did Jesus and Mohammed study, read? The Old Testament, (neither of them knew it, by the way), which was written FIRST in 800 BC (before that, for example, the Sumerians,Gilgamesh Epic). In the Old Testament, phenomena originating from nature were integrated as miracles or punishment, such as the flood, which is mentioned in all cultures, namely when the ice age had ended,

around 10500 B.C. the sea level rose by 140 metres, these areas were populated at that time. (By the way, 15,000 years ago, there were only 10 million people living on the entire planet). This is how the myth of Noah came about. These NATURAL PHENOMENA are said to have been made by God. Another one is the comet Halley. As I said, a little exaggeration here, a little exaggeration there, and there we have the proof of God. But back then people had a different understanding, a different picture of the earth, it was unexplored. After all, how many people died, went blind, because they tried different foods until they agreed on which ones they could eat and, of course, until they discovered the therapeutic properties of herbs? Today we know more.

Because as we know today, the dinosaurs were wiped out by a asteroid impact. Sodom and Gomorrah (ca. 3600 BC) have also been proven to have been destroyed by comet impact. And because of this event, hence this story of the Apocalypse, Absinthos. As in the Flood? As in Siberia in 1908? And finally: climate change also a work of God?

God became a man so that man might become a God!!!

Or, we are made in the image of God, so what exactly?(laughter).

———

There are three possibilities. We come from nothing and we go to nothing, we come from nothing and we go to paradise or hell, we come from nothing and we go to a parallel universe. Or, to put it more simply, we go where we come from. So what is this nonsense!!!

You are what you think you are!

My power is great, but at the same time insignificant, do you understand? You give value to everything, Homo sapiens! No matter what!

—

Do you know the travelling saviour?
The one who hops from galaxy to
galaxy and says: May I introduce
myself? Son of God! And you?

A millionth of a second directly after the Big Bang, the oscillations of gravity were already there, and all the other forces that act throughout the universe. They permeate everything, because everything is energy, in different forms.

This is the framework (of this universe) into which Homo sapiens was born. So they also have an effect on him and are perceptible to him.

There is no salvation,only knowledge.It is time that superstition came to an end.

Because in the Middle Ages, the world view prevailed that the earth was a disc and the sky was a vault, and they were afraid that the sky might come crashing down on them. The inquisitors (popes, patriarchs, etc.) wondered why we don't get dizzy when the earth spins, and they didn't wonder why the sea doesn't just pour out into space. Because to them, the earth was simply FLAT! Unbelievable, but true!

Man is not descended from apes,
he is one!!!

Who should learn to live with nature
again and not against it.

Jesus said that for real life you are
like birds. Are you not better than
them? Then why do you worry?
Believe and it will be given to you!
But who believes in it nowadays?
Not even the Pope and the
Patriarchs, not to mention the
3 billion simple believers. After

all, it is about faith.

Or it doesn't apply and his teaching
is just shit. So what is this nonsense!

(It also applies to the Muslims).

Buddha and Jesus were sensitive enough to perceive the vibrations of gravity. Each developed it according to his possibilities, thus the myth came into being, then the conviction and the faith, whereby Buddha is to be ranked higher, because he developed the highest power, that of the spirit and not that of the ordinary siddhi, namely that of the will, i.e. miracles.

But none of them knew that the earth is a planet, and the great Socrates did not know what lightning is and what a tectonic plate is (and neither did Jesus, Buddha and Mohammed), how could he, that is the knowledge of the last 200 years. A little hint, Zeus did not (laughter).Civilisation as we know it today was created in the last 100 years, are you aware of that Homo sapiens?

Who,when, where, what, knew what!

Or did they both "see" the same
God of this solar system (Mara,
Devil), one as a victim and the other
as a laughing victor? This would
explain a lot, wouldn't it? And
another question: Where were we all
5 billion years ago? The solar system
did not exist at all!
But the universe does!

LET THERE BE LIGHT!
God said it and it became light. Only
that HE had to say it twice. Once for
the universe (13,8) and once for the
solar system. Because, as we know,
the solar system came into being later
than the universe. It didn't work out
the first time.
Laughter. Or maybe four more
times? Earth, extinction of species,
human-like species and finally
Homo sapiens?laughter.

Buddhism is a philosophy, but it has applications in real life, different stages of development, up to the Buddha.

———

For it is not that the world needs
ONE saviour, Buddha, prophet, but
NONE at all. For it is the posturing
of Lucy for Lucy's sake.

Because the first beginning of
consciousness happens at the age
of 5 and 99% of people stay with
it until the end, some have a
second realisation and become
teachers and prophets, the
Buddhas have a third and are
called Buddha and God-Man, it's
as simple as that.

Do not be like sheep following
their leader, but become truly free
people. Adolf and Bonaparte
send their regards.

—

You can't combine Empedocles and
Darwin with virgin births. (Laughter)

Each one believes only in what he
has just stumbled upon in his
manifold wanderings, and yet
each boasts that he has found the
whole. *Empedocles*

So: Jesus, Buddha, Mohamed and
other divine representatives were
also on ODYSSEY. (Laughter)

Evolution of man,
evolutionary deities, so
simple.

We open up new dimensions and we
appoint the one who made it
possible as Buddha or God. It is as
simple as that.

Everything in nature strives for
perfection, you die with it, so why
not live with it?
For Σωτηρία=salvation,
redemption means in ancient
Greek: to be round,complete.

I tell you about the light that you
carry within you anyway.

I see prophets with their visions, all descendants of someone who was not a master. Masters with their miracles, with their ordinary siddhi, who were not buddhas, determine the faith of 5 billion people today. Absurd, isn't it? And Buddhas who have done nothing but perceive the conditions into which man is born and the vibration of gravitation that has been proved, the so-called music of life!!!

Reality is a product of our brain. It may be that we only perceive a simulation of reality, a pseudo-reality thanks to the eyes, because they are two globes that are so busy perceiving the visible world that afterwards one is hardly able to perceive one's own inner world, and through this we shape our reality. So faith determines what we are able to perceive as reality, because the essential is invisible. According to the motto, what I don't know doesn't make me hot: the universe and Einstein's explanation and the vibrations that Buddha was able to perceive and recognise their meaning. What you think is reality, so simple. Everyone is able to create and perceive his or her own true reality, by

to think into this state, or more simply to perceive the framework into which Homo sapiens was born, with everything, gravity, its vibrations and forces. This is then called enlightenment. The famous well-known γνωθι σαυτον (:know thyself), by Socrates. (Self-knowledge).

Is an axiom really correct?

And if not, then we live in a false reality that we have created ourselves as the end product of our imagination, our belief, because everything is invention (Epinoisi).Is this world satanic and ugly as an end product of our (Christian) faith? Interesting, isn't it? Homo sapiens.

It's like jumping from two-dimensionality to three-dimensionality. It's like a board game, everyone else moves on it and I see the three-dimensional hemisphere or the whole one that has formed in front of me, and everyone else sees the circle that has formed, but also sees that I see the sphere, periodically as in a sine curve, between these two dimensions.

We all come into this world to have
this experience, not to worship
anyone or to pay homage to any god.
It is as simple as that.

Buddha and Christ are actually saying the same
thing. A new awareness of true reality, only in
different words and terms.

It is different to be a great personality (Gandhi,
Mandela) and different to be truly alive
(Buddha, Jesus).

The great leap for us homines
sapiens happened 2500 years ago. It
was then that man became the centre
of observation and no longer nature.
Socrates, Buddha and Jesus (The
Kingdom of God is within you) and
all thanks to evolution.

Not the man Jesus, but Christ, the
consciousness, told about the
experience.

For an Australopithecus God is
not acceptable , as well as a
schizophrenic prophet.

How about this: Our energy (soul) was already existent in other universes, and when the possibility of Homo sapiens was given, it came here to have this experience of perception. That would explain the kingdom and the I-am-not-of-this-world, or nirvana. Not bad, is it? Until then, I have seen.

From another universe where all creatures can talk and communicate with each other and are vegetarians. No saviour, no promise, just harmony. A beautiful idea, isn't it?

—

Take a pencil, hold it vertically with the tip on a table and let it go. It falls in a different direction each time, this is called symmetry. (In physics, symmetry is the property of a system to remain unchanged after a certain change). So our universe also came into being in one direction, completely by chance with these particles, this mass, these forces. And then someone should tell me that I am not right about the frame.

Put me in the moment of the Big Bang and I'll create a new different universe for you. (Laughter)

Isn't it a mistake in thinking to say that we see the past of the universe up to the Big Bang?

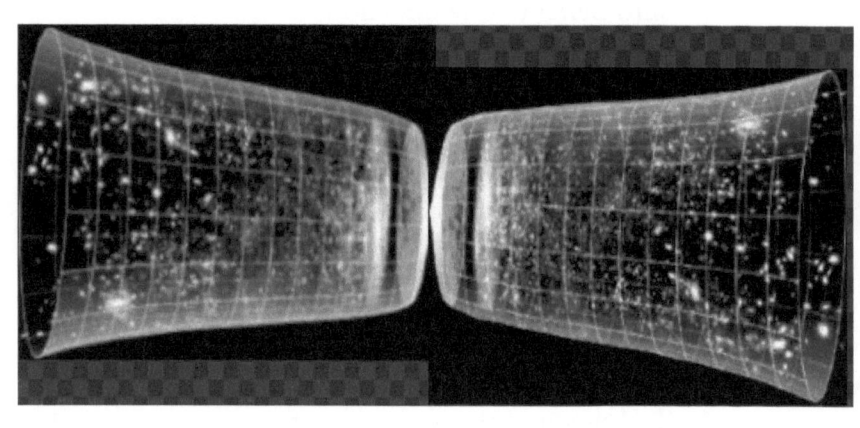

In the beginning, the universe was very small and dense, then there was the Big Bang, and then it BEGAN to expand.So when did our galaxy come into existence, if not at the very beginning? where was our galaxy at the beginning of the universe? We are the beginning!Or even simpler, what is the oldest structure in the universe? Our galaxy, 13.8 billion years old to be exact. So better explained, the oldest structure in the universe is our galaxy, and it is 27.6 billion years old, and the YOUNGEST galaxy is 13.4 billion years old, because that is how long it took light to reach us. Obviously, we are living in a black hole! At the Big Bang it is still being born! As the oldest star, galaxy from another universe through the black hole (white), as the youngest star with this age as a newcomer in our known universe. Therefore, physicists ask themselves: How is it possible that such a huge star (millions of times bigger than our sun and galaxies) was formed so early? Or even simpler: Is the whole universe enclosed in a black hole? Does time even exist, an error of mankind? I ask you, Homo sapiens!

If the physicists with the Webb telescope see the beginning or the limits of the universe, or stars and galaxies that don't belong there or that are older than the known universe, then I am right that we are living in a black hole.

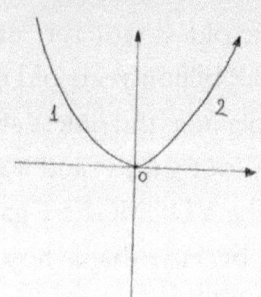

The universe shrinks
(1) and expands (2). At 0 is the black (white)
hole, the Big Bang. The view behind the mirror.
(Imagine an hourglass. Because after the
cosmological horizon of observation, space-time
curves and everything comes together at one
point,
(Riemann)). And this can repeat itself an infinite
number of times. So there are infinitely many
parallel universes, each time changing the rules,
constant renewal. One into the other and from
one universe into the other. Everyone thinks of
the black holes
(which, by the way, are gravity itself) inside the
system, but never outside. (The whole thing is
compatible with Einstein's wormholes). And,
that matter is transformed in the black holes and
it is not lost. Man is microcosm and
macrocosm, so he can also explode and expand
infinitely if he wants to. Because an orange is
the sun and the earth is a grain of rice 10 metres
away, and we're all on it (Munich to Berlin one
light year). That is the relation. Now, Homo
sapiens, you can more easily imagine expanding
over the whole earth. We are talking about the
possibility of HUMAN!

OR: One point. The before and the after of this universe and in between us, the Homines sapiens.

Light has been travelling towards us for 13.8 billion light years. A lot has happened in the meantime, perhaps it no longer exists, dark emptiness, may well be so. So we are ALREADY in the middle of an already dying universe. To put it more simply, what we see is a projection of the universe.

My greatest dream is to be allowed to see this monster called religious tradition collapse and the enlightened HUMAN emerge, constantly renewing itself!!!!

For when the Halley comet appeared, in the Palaeolithic period, it was seen as a radiant warrior, a legend from which the thunder god arose. Later it became God the Father Almighty, who even sent his son afterwards - a legend out of legend.

Homo sapiens and his tendency to declare natural phenomena to be God. Until then, the mother earth was worshipped (fertility goddess). For the world of gods and the form of society have changed from matriarchy to patriarchy, remnants of which are the goddess Athena and the Virgin Mary.

What do you think the moment was like when the first human being made the first observation and had the first thought about it? Plato's cosmos of ideas was born with it (something like the framework, I suppose).

By the way, you Homo sapiens can calculate your energy, because it is the speed of the rotation of the earth squared times your mass (weight) and when you explode, that is your released energy (Einstein). What is valid for the atom is also valid for humans, for rodents (laugh). This creates a convergence in the space-time continuum and if you are lucky, you can see into the future. It's as simple as that.

—

I am the reincarnation of the first
human being who made the first
observation and thought about it and
the last observation and thought
about it, all other contemporaries
only follow.

I am the king of rodents.
                    (Laughter)

So, I am the logical evolutionary
development of man, because now
mankind knows about the universe.
(Collectively).

Einstein knew how HE thinks and
I knew how HE feels.

Einstein understood it, explained it
and I experienced it, curved space.
Because I have reached the critical
density and I exploded, causing a
shock   or   gravitational   wave.

Unio mystica:

I entered and did not know where,
and I also remained without
knowledge, transcending all
knowledge. (...) Anyone who gets
there becomes quite mad about
himself. Everything he knew before
now seems infinitesimal to him. And
his knowledge grows so much that
he remains without knowledge,
transcending all knowledge.

Because what was I doing all this
time? Be empathetic.

So the question is, what is there outside the frame (UNIVERSE), such as the distant being (of Socrates) or simply NOTHING? Because a lot of stupidities have been written about virgin births, I find!

Our universe must be 10 times bigger than we know, can see, and there must be billions of parallel universes, all created by chance just like ours, and all of them will eventually cease to exist. Simply madness, isn't it Homo sapiens?

How many galaxies are already in front of us, we see the past but not the future, I mean since they must have formed BEFORE our galaxy (with flat universe), so how many galaxies

have already flown past us?
Interesting thought, isn't it, Homo
sapiens? Maybe a whole universe
already!

How many billions of galaxies, how
many billions of stars, how many
billions of planets, this number is
beyond imagination. Do you still think
that we are alone, Homo sapiens?

A little more history. Until the 19th
century, Europe had empires (emperor,
empress, etc.), then independent states
with fledgling democracies, then
dictatorships that introduced the term
homeland - and since then democracies
that unfortunately still use the term
homeland. The Australopithecus is
trying. Also in religions. He likes to try
things out! (laughter). But political
changes take a few years, religious
changes centuries. See Adolf, see
Christ.

Anyway, there are those who
perceive or those who do not
perceive.
By thinking into it, we may all
become perceivers.

What the perceiving person
experiences in an hour,
others do not experience in a
whole lifetime.

It is the path of Homo sapiens
from ignorance to knowledge
and at the same time it is the
"panda rei", (Heraclitus),the
path of education, formation,
cultivation, wisdom.

For Homer's narrative is man's
journey to himself, and Ithaca
is the arrival at the true man,
without gods and blinders.

Furthermore, if HE (GOD) sent His only Son, WHY has He (Son) not been heard in the WHOLE world at the same time and understood? As the saying goes: IN THE BEGINNING WAS THE WORD. Did HE send him like that, without the ability to make himself understood everywhere, but with the ability to perform miracles? It is simply absurd, and this also applies to all other messengers of God. And why wait 200,000 years, and in a forgotten language (Aramaic)?

I tell you, dear reader, because humanity has only been communicating with each other for a few thousand years and through this this consciousness has arisen and because now the idea of evolution exists. Now humanity is waiting for the one who will break through into this DIMENSION, we are talking on this our EARTH.

Maybe it will happen in the next millennium. I tell you, evolution will do its work until our sun no longer exists. Because Lucy's (the first known human-like being, who, by the way, is also said to have been created by our God) goal is to perfect itself, spiritually, physically and energetically. Each time a new dimension. Until everything disappears again into nothingness.

Because we know nowadays that in the last 700 million years, species have gone extinct five times, but some species has always survived and so the theatre went on. And NOW here we are, Homo sapiens.

Life on earth is comparable to a book of
10,000 pages, Homo sapiens is a few lines down on the right side of page 10,000, we are talking here about

very short time! Almost insignificant and we take ourselves so important and we are destroying everything, just madness!

We owe the cartography of the earth to the seafarers (maps from 3000 years ago, 1000 years ago and from 2022, today!) and the end of superstition to the merchants, because they developed further, opened new horizons, also spiritually, and spread the new ideas. And today we are mapping the universe! And this in the last 500 years.

The Cyclops myth tells of how the Greeks attributed the rough wall constructions, e.g. in Mycenae, to the Cyclops. They could not imagine that their own ancestors could move these huge stones and shift them so precisely.(So it's a processing). This precision reaches a climax in the Parthenon Temple. Here the grandiose development of civilisation can be seen.

Besides: the theory of rebirth is nice, but when did it start? With the Lucy (her peoples, her gods), with the dinosaurs, before the birth of the solar system or even before the Big Bang?

Something's not right, don't you think, Homo sapiens?

The story of Adam and Eve shows the journey from gatherer to cultivator/farmer(Abel and Cain, the eternal struggle) 10,000 to15,000 years before Christ. When Adam and Eve plucked the apple from the tree of knowledge/gnosis and ate it, namely when the agricultural revolution, (we only know since 1936 AD, the second being the industrial one) happened, they realised what a carefree time they had spent on earth, paradise, as gatherers (nostalgia, common property) and what toils in comparison a

Agriculture costs. So they complained, and out of that came the myth of Paradise Lost. (That is, an unfulfilled wish, wishful thinking). This is because resource wars began after sedentarisation.
It's as simple as that.

Where did it all take place? In the temperate zone, where the climate does not reach extreme temperatures.

Bless us the daily bread, the rice and the corn(laughter)

It is inevitable that man will destroy his environment because he will burn all fuels to the end, schizophrenia in all its glory, because time simply cannot be turned back and we cannot go back to the Middle Ages, Australopithecus has evolved, it is as simple as that.

It will either be the century of peace or of our destruction.

Who survived the dinosaurs? The rodents, the first mammals, common ancestors by the way, then this explosion of life, this diversity of all animal species and human-like species, Lucy first, then Neanderthal man, Denisova man, Hobbit, Archaic still living among us, and of course Homo sapiens. Since then, evolution has sought perfection in each species, with Lucy the triad (mental, physical, energetic), so-called Trinity of God, Empedocles sends his regards. Monsters gave birth to us and this will continue until all the dimensions physicists talk about (string theories, which strings are in us and pulsate in different frequencies) can be experienced, if we still have so much time as a species, before one day everything dissolves into NOTHING, even the universe (the frame), because even that has a beginning and an end.

So from time to time a few true human beings are born who achieve this breakthrough to a new dimension, to the end of time.

A bit of history: Pythagoras in 600 BC said the earth is round, Aristarchus in 300 BC that the earth revolves around the sun, no one believed them, Ptolemy then in 200 BC.

 that the earth was the centre of the cosmos, (hence the name earth, ground, fixed point, at that time mankind did not know that the earth was a planet like the others) and everyone believed in it, it fitted the will, for 1400 years, it had happened before the birth of the church, which FIRST acknowledged in 1992 A.D. that the earth was moving at all! Unbelievable but true. Stupidity had won and darkness still reigns, Homo sapiens.

Homo sapiens, I can understand men having a man as God, but women? The Lord Jesus, the Lord Buddha and as prophet the Lord Mohammed and the Lord God the Father. And where is the goddess Mrs Mother and why do women accept all this, I ask you, Homo sapiens.

It was only in 1924 that Edwin Hubble thought that that dot was a galaxy. Until then, mankind believed that our galaxy was the whole universe. Incredible but true. The whole of humanity.
Except Einstein. Not even 100 years ago, Homo sapiens.

Nature (Big Bang) is not paradoxical but paradoxical is our imagination/gnosis/image (knowledge) of the cosmos.

Is the earth God's work? If so, why does man not protect it? What kind of schizophrenia is this?

We develop ideas and ideas change us.

But what is meant by resurrection? Resurrection means the experience of oneness with this space- and timeless, infinite source, which we Westerners call ``God''. So the goal is not immortality(which, by the way, only exists in the minds of others), but the experience of the timelessness of our true being, which can manifest itself in very different forms. And that in the here and now, not after death. Which, by the way, does not exist, it is simply a transformation of energy. Because that is the true message of Christ. So become a true human being. So do not worship, but become.
So the meaning of existence is to be found in the here and now.

But unfortunately, nowadays everything is for pleasure, even bread and games, just like back then.

Basically, the whole thing is quite simple, LUCY, her descendants, her peoples and her gods.

Evolution and everything is possible. Or do you think that the first bacterium had an ego consciousness, and had it sacrificed itself to become oxygen? (Laughter)

There is a crowd in paradise. Or what does it look like there? On the left side the Muslims, on the right the Catholics, in the middle the Orthodox and next to them the Jews and the rest? (laughter). And what will the Hindus believe in when the holy Ganges dries up? (Which it will!) Glacier melt.

Let's clone an Australopithecus so we can see the work of God in all its glory. (Laughter)

 3.5 million years ago an Australopithecus, in 3.5 million years an evolutionarily evolved chimpanzee, will say I am the light! (laughter).

So much fuss for one bacterium. The world is crazy! (Laughter)

There must be billions of life forms in the universe. Since the whole universe has a single starting point, the same conditions for the emergence of life must have been present everywhere: Bacteria here, bacteria everywhere.

It's as simple as that, and everyone wonders if they are ALONE in the universe. (Laughter)

As we know, the soul travels, so what is stopping you, Homo sapiens, from travelling to another universe? This is a new horizon, IDEA.

Or what is the matter with all of you, Jews, Christians, and Muslims? You all want to give your minds to God! There is an alternative.

—

We are all here because Lucy wanted to reproduce, funny. It gets even funnier because now we also have saviours, Buddha and prophets, funny isn't it? It will be even funnier if we now appoint a single saviour as the only surviving species. (Laughter) Conclusion: I am available.

One invented cuneiform writing, the alphabet, the wheel, mathematics, air conditioning, one invented paradise and I invented travel to another universe. I tell you Homo sapiens, everything is invention except what one is able to perceive or feel.

What has been written, when, by whom, for whom? E.g.: About the mother of all monotheistic religions, Judaism. I mean the Old Testament. As you have already understood,

is totally wrong (Wrong base).
Notice that Jesus didn't even want to change one i in the Old Testament. And paradise is not even a Hebrew word, Persian.Do you understand what I mean Homo sapiens?

And because nowadays science has explained the biblical 10 plagues of Egypt and proved that they were the consequences of the volcanic eruption of Santorini around 1600 BC.

Does the universe have an evolutionary consciousness and created us, brought us forth? Does it think about itself? Because bacteria everywhere! Because nowadays DNA has been detected on a meteorite.

Christianitism, Islamism like Buddhism, capitalism etc. Australopithecus and all its: -ism.(Laughter)

Let us create a WORLD HOLIDAY to celebrate the END of WARS, something like May Day or better like SILVESTER, and with which the consciousness of humanity changes as far as the attitude towards war is concerned. The day of the end of the Second World War is suitable for this. ONLY in this way will it be possible to change consciousness! Imagine that those in power declare war again and no one goes, it's that simple, no one follows them. THAT would be the miracle. And not the fish and the wine.

Mein Kampf

World Holiday
8th May

Steinart

The drawing was made so that it becomes clear how fragile peace is.

Description from top to bottom: My Struggle, The Cross that Forbids the Tank, WORLD HOLIDAY
and 8th May. In the colours red and blue, that of blood and that of knowledge.

That is the IDEA.

PS: Why Germany?

I chose Germany to make this idea known because it would have a strong symbolic character for the whole WORLD, if Germany would move in this direction after all and introduce this holiday as the first country, then all other countries would follow suit, I am sure.

And perhaps future generations will experience this miracle.

Or the people simply start **celebrating** everywhere of their own accord instead of waiting for declarations from the states, then the states will also comply with the will of the people, a vivid example of this is the GDR. And then, finally, these two words, namely "Mein Kampf", will get a totally different meaning. Thus we transform the emblem of the Nazis into the emblem of **PEACE**.

OTHERWISE CONTINUE TO
ASSUME, HOMO SAPIENS,
THAT ...

Because one is a myth, the other is not. We are
talking about the same time period, 1800 B.C. to
800 B.C. I mean in Mycenae (Cyclops) is a
myth, and in Judea
(Abraham and Sarah) is the Old Testament.
Something is wrong, don't you mean Homo
sapiens?

And the Bible brought the shame of the body
into the world, e.g. in Tahiti (as late as 1778
AD) the society was matriarchal and the
missionaries destroyed it.

The act of love was deified by the Hindus
through the Kama Sutra, and the Jews
brought shame to the body(they stoned to
death because of it), and that is what both
Christians and Muslims believe. Just
madness. They just dragged everything
through the mud. Even in love, violence.

VISION 1

Free time. Just do nothing for two hours a week and donate the money you would otherwise spend. This leads to more solidarity, more consideration, more understanding for the situation of others, more love and simply makes this world more bearable, it's as simple as that. It is the attitude that counts. Two hours of doing nothing, simply resting, reflecting on what for and why, without any religious background (I mean, not for any community), without expecting any reward, just like that, simply being allowed to be a HUMAN being for two hours. Without any promise of paradise or anything else, without any reason, just being human, just reflecting on humanity and on oneself.

So one account number per country and for the whole world one superior account number, administered by all spiritual leaders of this world (Nobel laureates of peace). And Dalai Lama, (by the way, he wears leather shoes, he does NOT ask himself, otherwise he is a vegetarian. (Laughter)), first for the needy and then for all (e.g. through joint humanity-serving projects).

So ALL the citizens of a town give one person 1 euro and so he gets his starting capital (e.g. 100,000 euros) and this is repeated until all the citizens have a starting capital. No more lottery, no more gambling, but help for self-help. Everything goes on as before, everyone goes about their work and ALL citizens have MONEY. No more poverty and gambling. Practising charity. Solidarity and no one is envious any more. No elbow society but a new way of thinking and living together. Homo sapiens is as simple as that! And that is a new IDEA!!!

10,000 years ago we were not even 10 million, in 1900 AD already 2 billion, 10 years ago 7 billion and today 8 billion people. Are you aware of this, Homo sapiens?

VISION 2

In 100 years, none of today's babies
will be alive, but the madness will,
because Homo sapiens shapes and
forms his children that way, and it's
so easy to change that, in three
generations even. Stop treating them
like pets. So I propose that the world
organisation UNO chooses a
common WORLD LANGUAGE by
democratic vote, the other national
languages remain and the children
grow up bilingual everywhere. All
that is lacking is the will to do it.
Think of it as in ancient times when
Greek was the language of
intellectuals and philosophy, the
universal language, even the New
Testament was written in ancient
Greek, at that time ancient Greek
was considered natural, in the

Time of Jesus. At least 20,000 Greek words have been preserved in the English language and one third of the German language also consists of Greek words.

This universal language is to be enriched with Latin loanwords that are found in most other languages. No swear words, another level of communication, harmony. This creates a rich language with which to express oneself. It is the language of philosophy, medicine, physics and logic anyway. In addition, the Olympic Games regain their true meaning, which is to maintain peace and harmony. The Greek language invented many new words and proved to assimilate many words,

can absorb, integrate and develop over the course of millennia. And then the Tower of Babel would simply be history and all the faith that goes with it. Simply everything.

Besides: humanity has the same term for most things as well as for abstract ideas (e.g. chair, love, universe, etc.). I mean, some word is used for the corresponding terms anyway, so why can't we agree on a common mother tongue? Since all languages have the same description for the same things, and have done so for millennia, yes there are translations. Why do we behave so stupidly and not agree on an international
Mother tongue? I think it's idiotic to have so many different words for the same concepts. That's

It's madness to look for translation in the age of the internet. Instead, children should be brought up bilingually, with one international language and one national language. It makes sense just because of the functionality of dealing with each other. In the city of love (Paris) there is a monument with the text "I love you" in all languages and the tourists have their pictures taken in front of it, simply idiotic. We can keep our cultural diversity and still be united as a species, it's that simple. And all humanity can start under the same conditions, hence a universal language, e.g. ancient Greek. We have grammar and works! Then we can finally all build a common bridge for the whole of humanity.

Because the CHILDREN are like sponges, they absorb everything they are served, from Chinese to ancient Greek, both the oldest living languages by the way.And also because children are like matches that need to be lit, not barrels that need to be filled, so simple. And how would it be if children were taught all religions. And from a certain age, the children can then decide for themselves whether they want to choose a religion at all, and if so, which one. We are now talking about the education of free people. Because free people have the choice. We just have to agree. I also propose the abolition of the term HOMELAND (The term is not even defined) so that we all become cosmopolitan. And we move from patriarchy to matriarchy(Because of all the violence and it will be paradisiacal as well when the comparison to each other and the possession are gone e.g. Tahiti.So the women take over and the men become real people). First this and then the workers create their own company. Eachdivision its company for the whole country. The company provides its specialised people, who in turn negotiate from company to company, no more employees, absolute competition. Restructuring of the labour market and society, we are now talking about free people and everyone benefits. Better distribution of money.

Because sin, for example, in ancient Greek is called amartia and means: wrong goal. In this sense, there is no original sin.

This has been misunderstood and mistranslated, one word and it means so much. Since there is no original sin, we don't need a redeemer. Because he was a child of his epoch. It's as simple as that.So right goal, the lived experience, which is to be truly alive.

For he is risen, he has discovered his inner world, he is truly alive, that is how the whole thing is to be understood.
(Kingdom of God is within you).
And ONLY Mary Magdalene understood this, the other apostles did not.So the 4 Evangeliums are also wrong.

Christ, by the way, believed in communal ownership, the first Communist that is.(Laughter)

EPILOG

Pigeonhole thinking pervades all areas of contemporary man. He thinks in categories, as far as his political life is concerned in the party spectrum, as far as his religious life is concerned in the world religions, simply everywhere. Everybody opens his drawer, says his opinion and goes back in again, so everybody is right from his point of view of things, instead of collecting the essence, the best ideas and finding a reasonable common denominator.

Everyone opens their drawer, says what they have to say, and that's that, but that's no way to have a DIALOGUE. Drawer open, drawer closed. Simply madness, as if they were on rails like trains going nowhere. (STUCK). If we could change that and look for common solutions

then I would see a possibility that reason would prevail and true dialogue between true human beings would begin. Because as you, dear reader, have already understood, it is not a question of origin, but of education.

But I tell you, we develop ideas and they change us.

We are now talking about universal love and possibility man. And resurrection is in the here and now and not after death. This experience of the timelessness of our true being in the here and now is what we are meant to experience as long as we live. That is what it is all about, NOW. That's why I say everyone is wrong (shit paradise, karma). Because the rationale is simple, EVOLUTION.
And the goal of evolution, AGAPE.

Because Pangaea was once and will be again. And everything will be razed to the ground as if nothing had happened. No work of Homo sapiens, absolutely nothing.

PS:

The ways of feeling the heart are at the same time the keys that open the heart of the other. This can be perceived.

The fire that the body feels.

The sweet rustling in the heart.

The wave of the heart that gushes out, that also reaches the sky and shakes the universe.

When the wave of the heart embraces the other, envelops and caresses the other's body.

The attraction that fills the bodies, as the body is wiser.

The energy that fills space or spacetime.
For the perceiver, the space is homogeneous and full of energy.

The desire for the other body.
Ecstasy.

The explosion and expansion of
energy from multiple selves when
you are everywhere and nowhere.

When you feel like you are in a
minefield, perceiving the energy of
the other bodies. Because gravity is
the experience of compressed space.
(Because not even Buddha experienced
it like that).

When the soul performs miracles.
Or when the voice is heard in space-
time.

Also, the spiritual force that brings
thinking to a standstill in others.

When you stroke your cheek and
make a person move, you are the
master of your energy field.

All this is called love. And at the
same time they are siddhi. And if you
have experienced one of them, you
have already experienced your true
being.

Two-three last things:

So: What did God do for 13.8 billion years? He fondled his balls and he felt ALONE, poor thing, as an absolute being and needed company, poor thing.

He thought, FIRST after that, let's create some human-like species, see what happens. Now Homo sapiens is the only species left and lo and behold, GOD is GREAT. What a ridiculous God HE is.

Or what have WE created?

To the Devil, where are all those born before Christ, in Paradise or Hell? We are now talking about 200000 years of Homo sapiens.(Laughter).

A joke: What was God doing when he created the dinosaurs? He was training! (Also image?) I think HE has problems with his own image! (Laughter)

EVA you were banished from paradise, chased away and you want to go back there? LAUGHTER

The whole thing is comically tragic. All this because of the religiosity of Australopithecus. Think about it Homo sapiens.

Shit happens, Jesus is born, Buddha and Mohamed. (Laughter) Because all three did not know they were an Australopithecus, only Empedocles.And all three are proselytising.

So a new party: The biblical Communists with a new economic system: socialist-capitalist. A new way of thinking and working together.

A bold, impudent assertion plucked out of thin air is everything religious, so if you're going to exaggerate, then do it properly, please!
I am the saviour of the universe! For I can shape the cosmos! If not of the multiverse!
That statement says it all, doesn't it?
LAUGHTER.

I am a Buddha by profession, but my true vocation is to be the saviour of the universe.
(Laughter)

What's the matter, big Jesus? What do you mean, don't give me that glass? You're supposed to go to heaven! You should be happy!
(Laughter).

But if you believe in me, I will give you a new universe. Because the world will go up in flames. Tell all the people you see! Follow me! On to new life forms! Boundless and free!

These forces of the universe work on the earth as they do on us humans. The masters call it intuition. What vibrates is the water in us, 70% namely, (70% water on earth, 70% dark energy in the universe.
coincidence?). Some are able to perceive, to feel all these forces. Such people become
Called "enlightened", it's in us, around us, it's everywhere. So much ado about NOTHING. (Laughter) EUREKA!

For whatever fertile ground of knowledge is found, that is how analogous knowledge arises, e.g. Buddha and the Brahmins with their gods, their categories of human beings, rebirth and karma, that is how he was able to develop his ideas, the state of knowledge at that time, and I with Christianity, ancient Greece with its philosophers, in addition to that the

Knowledge of all religions, which
are simply passed on anew,(which
are nothing other than the
systematisation of morality, ethics),
that's how I also gained my
knowledge. Other gnosis
(knowledge) then, others nowadays,
but today we know more. Because
everything is epinoisi(:what you
make up) on the altar of evolution.

Which is better? Paradise or a new
universe that you can shape
however you want! And every
homo sapiens becomes the saviour
in his universe! Tempting, isn't it?
(Laughter).

All those mentioned are my brothers!

There is no one out there who can judge,
do you understand Homo sapiens?

Because all religions are children of
the agricultural revolution. It's as
simple as that, Homo sapiens.

As if the planet animates us and the soul is only on loan and that's a new idea.

So Homo sapiens, you practise charity, love of your neighbour (without blinkers),but also leave the door open a bit for another universe, where do you see a problem there?

In the end, dear reader, it's all just an idea, it's as simple as that.

There is hope, the rodents will survive climate change again and maybe also an asteroid impact. The main thing is that the planet survives, as it did with the dinosaurs, and in 65 million years we humans will be around again, because that's how long evolution takes. Damn it, back to square one (laughter). With the same search, the same questions, the same myths, the same evolution. We can even all enjoy the end of humanity together. So don`t worry be happy.